A QUESTION AND ANSWER STORYBOOK

Why Does Popcorn Pop?

and other kitchen questions

by Catherine Ripley

illustrated by Scot Ritchie

Owl

Why Does Popcorn Pop? and other kitchen questions

Owl Books are published by Greey de Pencier Books Inc.,
P.O. Box 53, 370 King St. West, Suite 300, Toronto, Ontario M5V 1J9

The Owl colophon is a trademark of Owl Children's Trust Inc.
Greey de Pencier Books Inc. is a licensed user of trademarks of Owl Children's Trust Inc.

Distributed in the United States by Firefly Books (U.S.) Inc.,
230 Fifth Avenue, Suite 1607, New York, NY 10001.

We acknowledge the generous support of the Canada Council
for the Arts and the Ontario Arts Council for our publishing program.

Special thanks to the following people for their help with this book: Dr. Randall C. Brooks,
National Museum of Science and Technology; *Chickadee* Magazine; Bill Diehl-Jones, University of Waterloo;
Lizann Flatt; Dr. Helen Graves Smith, National Museum of Science and Technology; Leslie Huffman,
Ontario Ministry of Agriculture; Dr. Bill James; Dennis Klem, Inglis Limited; Dr. Richard E.C. Layne;
Ontario Arts Council; Gordon and Marion Penrose; and Bruce Ripley. And once again, thank you to Sheba, Kat,
Trudee, Mary and Scot for making the words and pictures really pop . . . sizzle . . . and bubble!

DEDICATION

**For Owen, Phoebe and Robin — my beautiful,
sparkling (sometimes grumpy!) kids — with thanks for making
your own lunches, folding laundry, doing dishes, etc. etc.**

Cataloguing in Publication Data

Ripley, Catherine, 1957–
Why does popcorn pop? and other kitchen questions

(Question and answer storybook)
ISBN 1-895688-70-1 (bound) ISBN 1-895688-71-X (pbk.)

1. Science – Miscellanea – Juvenile literature.
I. Ritchie, Scot. II. Title. III. Series: Ripley,
Catherine, 1957 – . Question and answer storybook.

Q163.R55 1997   j500   C97-930536-5

Design & Art Direction: Mary Opper

Also available:
Why is Soap so Slippery? and other bathtime questions
Do the Doors Open by Magic? and other supermarket questions
Why do Stars Twinkle? and other nighttime questions
Why is the Sky Blue? and other outdoor questions

**Children under the age of 5 should eat foods like popcorn
only with supervision, to prevent the chances of choking.**

Printed in Hong Kong

A B   C   D   E   F

Contents

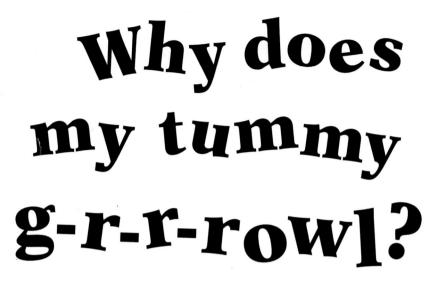

Why does my tummy g-r-r-rowl?

It's air rumbling around inside you. Inside your body, your stomach and intestines are always moving. When you eat, the movement mashes your food into soupy goop that your body can use to feed itself. But what happens when there is no more food left to mash up? Your stomach and intestines push around the air inside. Rumble, grumble.

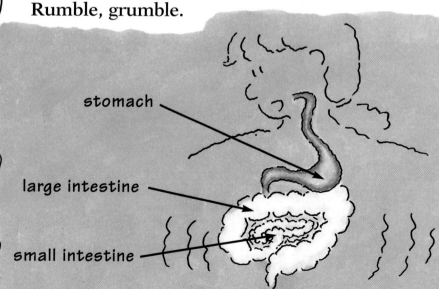

stomach

large intestine

small intestine

Why does popcorn pop?

Popcorn kernels are hard on the outside. But on the inside they are soft and a little bit wet. When you heat up the kernels, the water inside heats up too. It turns into a puff of hot steam that's trapped inside the kernel. The steam pushes from inside until the kernel explodes! The hard outer coat bursts open and the kernel turns inside out. Pop!

Children under the age of 5 should eat foods like popcorn only with supervision, to prevent the chances of choking.

Why are peaches fuzzy?

To protect the peach. All kinds of fruit — smooth apples, bumpy oranges, prickly pineapples and fuzzy peaches — have skin to help them stay healthy. Each type of skin keeps out insects or sickness or whatever it is that might hurt that kind of fruit. For example, peach fuzz stops a sickness called brown rot from touching the peach skin and rotting the fruit. The fuzzier the peach, the better!

Why does dish soap bubble so much?

Because there's more soap than dirt. When soap and water mix together, they make a film. It traps bits of dirt and slides them off the dirty dishes. But if there's more soap than dirt, the extra soap film traps bits of air. Soap film with air inside makes bubbles! The people who make dish soap know that we like lots of bubbles, so they put in a lot of extra soap. Lots of soap means you get tons of bubbles.

How does the fridge keep food cold?

compressor

By taking out the heat. The refrigerator has a long pipe in its walls. A motor, called a compressor, pumps special stuff through the pipe. The stuff collects the heat from inside the fridge where the food is. Then the fridge lets out the heat into the kitchen. By taking away the heat, the fridge keeps everything inside cool and frosty.

Why do onions make you cry?

Because you've cut them open. Like all things, onions are made up of molecules, tiny bits so small you can't see them without a powerful microscope. When you peel or cut an onion, extra strong, smelly molecules form, break away from the onion and float up to sting your eyes. Your eyes make tears to wash them away.

What makes food sizzle?

Dancing water drops! There is water inside food. When you put it in a hot pan, the water comes out in tiny drops. As soon as they hit the hot pan, the drops dance around, exploding into little puffs of steam. Dancing and exploding, they make little waves in the air that travel to your ears as a sizzling sound.

Why does garbage smell?

There must be food rotting in there. That means that tiny, tiny creatures called bacteria are breaking down the food. As they work on the food, some of them let out a smell. Pee-yoo! Good thing, because eating rotten food can make you sick.

Where does glass come from?

From the beach! That's because glass is made from sand. Sand is put in a really hot furnace with some other stuff, and it melts. Glass-makers take the red-hot liquid and shape it — carefully. When the glass cools down, it can harden into drinking glasses, or windows, or sunglasses, or . . .

Why do lemons make you pucker?

Because they are so sour. When you put lemon in your mouth, saliva takes the sharp juice to the taste buds inside your tongue. Taste buds send a message to your brain saying, "Too sour!" Your brain sends back a message to wash away the juice with more saliva. The saliva goes all over as your mouth squeezes and twists and . . . puckers!

Why do ice cubes crack?

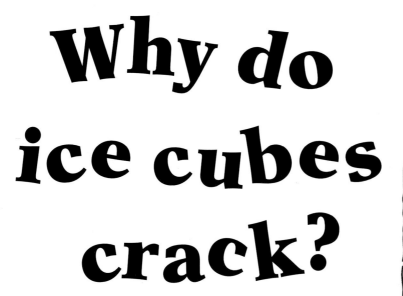

They're trying to shrink! When water freezes, it gets bigger and lighter. As soon as you put an ice cube in a drink, the outside of the cube wants to turn back into water. So the cube tries to shrink — quickly! The shrinking squeezes hard on the inside of the ice cube and, all of a sudden . . . the inside part goes crack!

How does blowing on food cool it off?

When you see steam rising from hot food, it's because heat is coming out. The steam acts like a blanket that helps keep the heat in. The faster you blow the blanket of steam away, the faster the heat can leave the food, and the faster the food cools down. Puff, puff, puff — yum!

Kitchen Bits

A special strip of metal inside your toaster makes your toast pop up. The heat makes part of the strip get bigger and bigger. The strip triggers a spring. The spring lets go of the bar the toast is sitting on. And up POPS your toast!

A long time ago, there was no electricity to run fridges. How did people keep their food cold on a hot summer day? They put it in an "ice box" with a big block ice. The ice was cut from lakes or rivers in the winter and stored in sawdust to keep it frozen.

Is it sugar or salt? It's hard to tell without tasting. Sugar is sweet because it comes from plants, like sugarcane and sugar beets. Salt is a mineral that is dried out of sea water or is dug out of mines underground.